FINDING MY

Misty Dearing

ISBN 979-8-89130-130-6 (paperback)
ISBN 979-8-89130-131-3 (digital)

Christian Faith Publishing
832 Park Avenue
Meadville, PA 16335
www.christianfaithpublishing.com

All scripture cited is from the NIV (New International Version) Bible translation.

Printed in the United States of America

This book is dedicated to the four loves of my life—Tom, Josiah, Eli, and Micah—and to Andrea, who has helped me navigate the past and present as well as give me hope for my future. Thank you; I wouldn't be who I am without you!

I also want to say a special thank you to my friend, Sharon, who spent many hours praying over this book.

PROLOGUE

Consider it pure joy whenever you face trials of many kinds because you know that the testing of your faith produces perseverance.
—James 1:2–3

For God so loved the world that He gave His only begotten son that whosoever believes in Him will have everlasting life.
—John 3:16

When I look back over my life, I see trauma, heartache, and a whole lot of things that should never have happened to me. But I also see the many incredible ways in which God walked with me (or carried me) every step of the way. He is so faithful! He is who the Bible says he is. He is the same yesterday, today, and forevermore. In my loneliest times, I was never alone. In my saddest times, he wept with me. In my happy times, he rejoiced with me. Over the course of the last few years, he has been teaching me how he sees me, how unconditional and how abundant his love is for me, and how to find joy. This book is not a representation of all the bad that can happen in life. Instead, it is a story of love—God's love—and his redeeming power to save and bring joy!

Heavenly Father, I pray over each soul that reads these words. I pray that you will speak through me. Thank you for your faithfulness, mercy, grace, unconditional love, and joy! In your precious name, amen.

CHAPTER 1

I have told you these things, so that in me you may have peace. In this world you will have trouble. But take heart! I have overcome the world.
—*John 16:33*

Train up a child in the way he should go, and when he is old he will not depart from it.
—*Proverbs 22:6*

The farm was a happy, peaceful place full of love, laughter, and learning about God. Granny and Papa were in their mid-forties when I was born. I was the first grandchild. They were part of everyday life for my first three years. When I was little, it seemed the farm was huge. There was the farmhouse, a garage, a large pole shed, the small pig barn, the cow barn with a milk house attached, the hay barn, and a small one-bedroom house. My mom had grown up in the main house with three sisters and a brother. The small house was built when my mom was a little girl. It was built by my papa and his brothers for their parents to live in their late years. This little house is where I came to live after I was born. I have memories of being that 2 1/2 year old waking up in the morning and running across the driveway to see Granny and Papa, have pancakes for breakfast, and then follow Papa out to the barn.

As I grew up, I would spend weekends, school breaks, and at least a month every summer with them. This was my happy place. Granny taught me how to cook, bake, and play cards. Papa taught me how to drive a tractor and help bale hay. They both taught me the love of Jesus and what he did for me on the cross. I helped feed animals, I played in the mud with the pigs, and I helped in the garden. Granny and I rode bikes together and took walks in the woods and collected rocks from the gravel pit. We watched game shows and colored. It was the place I felt safest in the world.

Although Granny and Papa have both gone home to heaven, the farm remains in the family as my mom bought the four-acre homestead. The house has changed in many ways since she moved in. A couple of things that are significant to me that I miss from how Granny and Papa had it are a large picture in the living room of an angel watching over children crossing a bridge and a hand-painted plate that Papa and I had done together one summer that had hung on the wall in the kitchen. I've often thought about that picture in times when I've needed comfort. Even though these things are gone, I'm so grateful that it's still a place I can go where I feel loved, safe, and comfortable.

Through this farm and these people, I fell in love with the great I Am. This foundation is how I made it through the many struggles that life has thrown my way. Jesus never said that life would be easy or that we'd always be happy. In fact, he specifically said, "In this life you will have troubles." The good news is he also promises to see us through all the troubles. He will never leave us or forsake us. We're all human. We all have hurts. We all fall short. But I have more good news—we are all forgiven! Perspective in this life is crucial. One of the things I've had to learn is that unfortunately, people who are hurting tend to hurt others. Once we understand that, it helps us forgive others and ourselves. It does not excuse bad behavior or take away the hardship we've felt because of it. However, it does give a measure of compassion not only for others but for ourselves. Through Christ, there is no condemnation but a spirit of love! I hope as you read this book, you will see how I've found healing, growth, and even joy because of the love of Christ. Thank you for taking this journey with me!

Lord, I ask that you will speak through these words. I ask that whatever it is you have for me and for those reading, we would be able to hear your voice through all the chatter in life. There is a reason you've given me the desire to write these words. Please use them for your glory. Amen.

CHAPTER 2

Jesus wept.

—John 11:35

The Lord Himself goes before you and will be with you; He will never leave you nor forsake you. Do not be afraid, do not be discouraged.

—Deuteronomy 31:8

It was the end of fall in 1979. I was 3 1/2 years old. My dad got a job in Minneapolis, so we packed up the little house on my grandparents' farm and moved to an apartment in that city. It was in this apartment that the sexual abuse by my dad began. I was one of those little kids that never wanted to wear clothes, so I ran around in underwear a lot, which is very normal. Due to his own mental illness and the hurt he'd suffered as a child being molested by his stepfather, he couldn't control the urges he felt to touch me inappropriately. He groomed me to think this sort of thing was normal between a daddy and a daughter. However, he also made sure to tell me that it was a very big secret because daddies and daughters don't tell anyone. If they did, it wouldn't be special.

I remember once when I was in just my underwear hearing a knock on the door. I opened the door to see my uncle (my dad's brother). He was a silly, goofy guy. When he saw me standing there without clothes on, he took out a pen and drew circles around my nipples, the shape of a nose around my belly button, and a smile under that. I thought it was so funny and went to show my mom. She definitely did not think it was funny; she was angry! It was confirmation in my young mind that Daddy was right; I should not tell

3

her about the things he and I did. I didn't want to get in trouble, and I didn't want to get him in trouble.

Right before kindergarten began, we bought a small trailer house in a small town about an hour south of Minneapolis. It was there that I started school, met a fun friend across the street, my mom met a close friend, and my dad worked for a couple of years. My mom's friend had kids my age, and we played and shared meals together often. When we were both about age seven, one of the little boys pulled his pants down and asked me to touch him. I remember feeling very strange about this because I thought it was only something daddies and daughters did. I ran away and later told my dad about it. He was so proud of me for not doing it, and I loved that feeling it gave me to make him proud. Unfortunately, my "reward" came in the form of pleasuring him. As I look back, all I see is a confused little girl desperately wanting her dad's love.

Jump ahead to summer of 1984. I was eight years old. We bought a different trailer house out in the country in the next small town over. We had one close neighbor and a few others that were spread out about a mile. The closest neighbors had two boys that were five to ten years older than me. These neighbors proved to be my saving grace on many occasions over the next five years. My dad stopped working, so my mom worked all the time—daytime as a florist, nights as a server, and weekends at a pizza place doing several different tasks. There were really good things about living in that community. My aunt and uncle and two little cousins (who I adored) lived there. I could walk from school to either their house or the flower shop. I met my closest childhood friend. And the nearby bike trails were awesome, giving me hours of biking enjoyment.

Because my mom worked so often, I was alone with my dad much of the time. From the outside, it looked like a beautiful way to grow up. I went fishing, boating, hunting, bowling, and to bingo with my dad. He taught me about cars, Star Wars, animals, and how to cook. Unfortunately, he also taught me about sex and (what he said) men want in a woman. He taught me that if women aren't what men want, men will leave. He taught me that my interests don't matter because I am here to serve men. Almost every day from age eight to ten, he touched me and made me touch him. The sad thing is at the time, I thought I was special because of it.

The older I got though, the more it didn't feel right. I started spending more and more time at the neighbor's house. The mom there was a stay-at-home mother, the dad was really nice, and the two boys would play games with me. They were a musical family, so there was always guitar playing and songs being sung. Most importantly, they were a Christian family, so there was prayer. It was a safe, calm, normal, happy place to be.

I also started spending more time with my best friend at her house. She lived in the country too but on the other side of town. She had horses which we rode frequently, and her mom stayed home due to health issues. Her mom was so loving and kind. Her stepdad also was loving and kind, not to mention so funny!

From the outside, it seemed like a pretty normal, happy childhood. No one knew that just beneath the surface, I was extremely lonely, sad, and very confused.

Father, if the readers of this book have experienced these same types of things, will you please do a work in their life like you did in mine? I lift up any who have suffered these things and ask that you would wrap them in your arms, give them peace and healing, and help them to see themselves through your eyes. Thank you for this person, Lord! I know without a doubt he or she is precious in your sight! I love you, Abba! In your precious name I pray, amen.

CHAPTER 3

Does God listen to their cry when distress comes upon them?
—Job 27:9

You will pray to Him and He will hear you.
—Job 22:27

One evening a couple of months before my thirteenth birthday, my dad wanted the three of us to go out to dinner. Mom and Dad fought about it because there really wasn't enough money to go. Dad won, and while we were eating, he dropped a bomb on us. He said we were moving to New Mexico, he was going to go ahead of us to find a house and a job, and then we'd come in a couple of months. My mom said absolutely not! She had work, I had school and friends, we didn't know anyone there, and she just was not willing to move away from her family. I sat and watched in fear as they argued about what the plan would be. That night before bed, my mom told me not to worry, we weren't going anywhere, and everything would be okay.

Two months went by, and nothing more was said. It was all but forgotten. Then one day after school, I went to the flower shop and from there Mom and I arrived home to find a note on a yellow piece of paper from my dad. It said that he had gone to New Mexico for a job and to find our new home and that he'd let us know when we should come. I'll never forget my mom sobbing and the feeling I had inside of life spinning out of control. She told me we weren't going, and she'd be filing for divorce. I made a vow to her that I would take care of her.

Life just kept spinning out of control for the next few months. My mom's high school sweetheart was suddenly back in the picture. Then they broke up and another man was in the picture. Then the high school sweetheart was back again. My mom started drinking more and going out at night. Then my dad called and asked me to come visit him in New Mexico. I was glad to go. Little did I know a nightmare was about to happen.

Father, I know many have suffered the divorce of their parents, the introduction of stepparents, or even the death of parents. I am not alone in this. You are a father to the fatherless and so much more. Remind us of this when loneliness sets in. Remind us that you are always there!

CHAPTER 4

*I cry out to you, God, but you do not answer. I
stand up but you merely look at me.*
—*Job 30:20*

*And we know that in all things God works for the good of those
who love him, who have been called according to his purpose.*
—*Romans 8:28*

His trailer house is located way out in the desert with no
other homes around it. It smells of old ashtrays and smoke.
There's no air, and it's very hot. He leads me to a bedroom
with brown carpeting. There is one small window up high, no cur-
tain, no doors on the closet, nothing on the walls, and no furniture
except an old, stained mattress with no bedding on it. He says, "This
is your room." He then backs out and locks me in from the other
side. I don't really understand what is happening. I try to open the
door, bang on it, and yell at him to tell me what's going on, but there
is no answer.

Hours and hours pass. I think it's the next day before he comes
in. He has a glass of water and a piece of bread. He tells me I've
gotten chubby, and he's going to fix that because no man wants a
chubby girl. Then he walks out again and locks the door.

It's hard to figure how much time passes before he comes in
again. This time, he isn't wearing any clothes, and he makes me take
mine off too. He goes further with me than he ever has before. I
wonder where God is in this. I think a lot about that picture in my
grandparents' living room of the angel watching over the kids and

wonder where my angel is. I wonder how long this will go on. I wonder if I'll die here.

The next few days continue to be the same—locked in a room, naked, hot, one slice of bread and a glass of water each day, being let out only to go to the bathroom with him watching, and him coming in to pleasure himself and "teach" me things once a day.

Then he opens the door, throws in one of his shirts, and asks me to come eat spaghetti with him. I was so very hungry that I put on the shirt and went to the living room. I ate the small portion he gave me and watched TV. When he got up and went to the kitchen, I ran out the door. I ran as fast as I could, but it wasn't fast enough. Pretty soon he was in the car, driving right next to me, and he had a gun. I gave up and got in the car.

Once we were back, he ripped the shirt off me and locked me in the room again. This was when I started thinking that maybe my mom didn't want me anymore because how could she not know what was going on? Why hadn't she called to check on me? I huddled in a ball in the corner of the room facing the door trying to stay vigilant for when he'd return. I thought about how I could knee him in the privates or poke his eyeballs out. I scratched at my skin until I bled just to keep myself awake. Then after a while, thoughts started to intrude of total escape—taking my own life.

At some point (I think it was day 6 or 7), I had given up. I was letting myself sleep sometimes. I woke up to the phone ringing. Then came the sound of my door being unlocked. He told me my mom was on the phone, and I was allowed to talk to her only if I told her I was having fun and everything was great. He told me in no uncertain terms that if I said anything other than that, he would kill her, and it would be my fault. I did as I was told, but something tipped her off (mother's instinct perhaps) because within a few hours, the police were knocking on the door to do a welfare check. I told them the same thing I told my mom out of fear he would kill her. I felt the need to protect her and take care of her at all costs. The police left, but the next day, one of the officers was back. He asked me if there was anything wrong and if I wanted to go home to my mom. I said there was nothing wrong, but I did want to go home. He got my mom on the phone, and I was on a plane home shortly after. When I got home, the time in New Mexico was not spoken of. Later in life, I learned that I blocked it from my memory in order to survive the trauma. Life went on, but my joy was gone.

God, you are the King of kings and the Lord of lords! There is no one like you! This experience was the worst thing that has ever happened to me. I know there are other kids who have experienced similar circumstances. We grow up with a wound inside us that only you can fill. My prayer for those who experience things like this is that they will see that it wasn't that you weren't there, couldn't hear them, and/or weren't listening! Absolutely not! You were right there in that situation weeping about what your beloved son or daughter was going through. You gave each of us a free will, and we live in a fallen world. But the good news is that you use ALL THINGS for our good! You can make the ugliest experience turn into something beautiful. Thank you for that promise! Amen.

CHAPTER 5

But you, God, see the trouble of the afflicted; you consider their grief and take it in hand. The victims commit themselves to you; you are the helper of the fatherless.

—Psalm 10:14

Y ou are the God who sees me.

—Genesis 16:13

This chapter probably won't make sense to most as it seems like the choices I made next would not be the choices of someone who had been kidnapped and sexually abused just three years earlier. I want to remind you though that I had blocked it from my memory as if it had never happened.

Summer of 1992, my dad told me he was getting married to a woman who had two teen daughters. They wanted to meet me, and he wondered if I would go on a road trip with them to Maryland to see her family. I quickly agreed because things in Minnesota weren't going very well. There had been a boy I had been dating off and on. He had invited me to his house to have dinner and watch a movie with his family. The opportunity to spend time with a happy family, with parents that were still together, very much appealed to me. I accepted, and he picked me up.

When we entered his house, I was confused because no one in his family was home. He said they were picking up food and would be back soon. We went up to his bedroom, and as we entered, he shut the door and locked it. I didn't know it then but I've learned since that the minute I heard the door shut and the lock click, I went into freeze mode as part of a PTSD episode. He began kissing me and touching me. He wanted to have sex. I said no. It happened anyway. I turned sixteen a few days later, got my driver's license, and then my mom got a DUI and lost her license for thirty days. So I had to drive her everywhere. Suffice it to say I was ready for some sort of change.

When I met my new stepsisters, it was like we'd known each other our whole lives. We really clicked and had so much fun together. Their mom was nice, my dad seemed really happy, and the road trip was a blast. So by the end of summer, I was enrolled in high school there and moved in with them. Right away I became very popular. I had never had many friends in Minnesota, but in New Mexico, it was quite the opposite. I loved it there!

I loved it…for about three months. That's when inappropriate sex talk between my dad and his wife started at the dinner table like it was a normal conversation topic. It wasn't healthy sex education for teenagers or the protective guidance of a parent. Then I woke up one day on the couch to him touching me under my shirt. From that day on, I lived with my boyfriend at his sister's house. I was a 4.0 student, held two jobs, tutored, and went to church. I also drank a lot! I wanted to do the right things, be the best me I could be, and make people proud. The problem was I was so confused, angry, and scared that I didn't know up from down. I tried to go back to what Granny and Papa had taught me about God. I prayed more, went to church every Sunday, and even got baptized. At the time, I felt like nothing I did was right or good enough, and I didn't deserve God's forgiveness. As I look back, I see how God was right there with me, protecting me, loving me, giving me strength and energy, and working in my heart.

For months my dad would follow me—stalk me. I'd look in my rearview mirror, and there he'd be. Sometimes he'd drive away when I stopped somewhere, but other times, he'd get out of his car and call me names or put me down in some way. Then one day about three weeks before school was to end, the police showed up at my door. They said my dad was requiring me to come "home," and because I was under the age of eighteen, I had to go. They waited while I packed my things and then followed me to his house. When

I arrived, I told him I would go back to Minnesota before moving back in with him. He said that was fine. My mom was all for that.

Unfortunately, when the school was called, I was told my credits would not transfer because there were only three weeks left. If I left before completing the school year, I'd have to repeat eleventh grade. So I did what I had to do to finish the school year and then was on the first plane to Minnesota. One of the things he required me to do was tell the pastor of the church that I was repentant of my ways. My dad also went so far as to say that he and I should sing a duet at church the last Sunday before I left so that everyone would see that he and I were okay. At this point, I did whatever I was told. I remember standing in front of that congregation singing "Leaning on the Everlasting Arms" thinking what a lie I was a part of.

Father, your word says that you see us. I truly believe that means far more than just a simple look. I believe you see every tiny part of us. You know our hearts and our minds; you know our innermost thoughts. I had a lot of shame for many years because of the wrong decisions I made. I now know that you saw me—you saw the little girl hurting inside, you saw the teenager trying to live right and do the right things, and you saw all the confusion that life threw my way. Thank you, Father, for being with me each step of the way, for forgiving all the missteps, and for welcoming me over and over again into your loving arms!

CHAPTER 6

It is the Lord, your God, you must follow, and him you must revere.
Keep his commands and obey him; serve him and hold fast to him.
—*Deuteronomy 13:4*

In those days Israel had no king; everyone did as they saw fit.
—*Judges 21:25*

Upon my return to Minnesota, because my mom had moved to the northern part of the state to be with her high school sweetheart, I joined them there. Although I tried to make the new living situation work, I was too angry at the world, and I didn't want to spend my senior year in a new school. So it was decided I would move in with my aunt and uncle back in my hometown to finish high school.

I was able to graduate early (January instead of June). At that point, I moved to a larger suburb of Minneapolis to start life on my own. A wealthy couple who lived on a large lake hired me to be a nanny to their children. It felt like I was living in a dream! I had my own apartment attached to their multimillion-dollar home, was getting paid a high salary, had minimal bills, and had my own jet ski, allowing for alone time on the water. It was a life of privilege I had never known was even possible. I spent quite a bit of time with longtime friends, one of whom would later become my husband.

This friend and I met when I was thirteen. He was dating my older sister at the time. He was eight years older than me, and I looked up to him like a big brother. He was enrolled in a Christian college and told me his dreams of being a youth pastor, traveling the world on mission trips, and serving God however he could. When I was fifteen (and he was twenty-three), we briefly dated. My sister put an end to that as soon as she found out. At the time I was very angry. I didn't see anything wrong with it. As I look back now, I see so much wrong with a twenty-three-year-old volunteer youth pastor wanting to date a fifteen-year-old.

We kept in touch, and during a long friendly talk on my couch one evening, he asked me to marry him. Although I didn't love him in a romantic way, I said yes. I was caught up in the life he was promising me. At eighteen, I thought this was my chance to have a Christian marriage like my grandparents.

Within two weeks, depression hit severely. I wanted to die. In the middle of the night, I laid down on my cold bathroom floor, started taking pills, and begged God to take me. God had other plans for my life, however. He appeared to me as if in a vision (maybe it was an angel). I heard him speak clearly. He told me to stop what I was doing, that he had a plan for my life, and that he loved me. I got up, made myself vomit, went to bed, and never told anyone what had happened. My life was then consumed by work and wedding plans.

We were married in May 1996. It wasn't the wedding that I had dreamed about. I hated the dress, my sister wasn't there, the flowers were fake, the reception was in an ugly church basement, and my new husband didn't allow one of my best friends to come to the reception.

The plan moving forward was to go to South Dakota where he would get a seminary degree, and we'd serve in a church there together. However, he decided he was not going to go to college and instead he'd just start candidating for positions.

The first one we applied for was in Wisconsin. We went there and met the people of the church. There was a big party for the youth group at a lake home where we all played volleyball, swam, shared conversation, and ate. Everything seemed lovely. They said they'd let us know. About a week later, there was a phone call from the pastor. He asked for my husband, and I told him he was out of town on a business trip. He asked me to have my husband call him. I wanted to know if we had been chosen, so I asked. He said he really needed to talk to my husband. His tone was ominous, and I knew something was wrong. I asked him to please tell me what was going on. He then told me that a couple of teenage girls came forward after the church party. They told the pastor that my husband had made inappropriate comments to them, and they felt very uncomfortable. He also asked if I knew about a relationship where my husband had been dating a teenager while he was volunteering in youth ministry. I said yes and informed him that I was that teenager. He asked me not to tell my husband yet—that he'd like to talk to him. I said I understood.

Later when my husband told me that we did not get the position, I asked why. He said it was ridiculous because it was all because he and I had dated when I was young. I asked if there was any other reason to which he said no. This was the first time I knew he was lying to me. Yet I was the submissive wife that did not challenge her husband. I said nothing.

We never candidated for another position. Instead, he got a job in the IT field and volunteered with the youth group at our church.

Lord, I worship you! Even when our intentions are good, sometimes we do things that are outside of your will. We can be so deceived into thinking that something will honor you that we don't even listen to what you may be saying to us. Then when deep disappointment comes, we cry out to you asking why. If we had just rested in your presence and listened for your soft, still voice, we wouldn't be in the position of asking why. I wanted so badly to have my grandparents' marriage and serve you the way they did that those things became idols. Instead of talking to you directly to seek your will, I did what seemed right in my own eyes. This chapter of my life shows me, and hopefully will show others, that even good plans can become idols. We need to ask YOU if it's your will—and then wait and listen. Thank you for using all things for our good and your glory. It's a mercy and a grace we don't deserve yet you freely provide.

CHAPTER 7

You may ask me for anything in my name and I will do it.
—John 14:14

Trust in the Lord with all your heart and lean not on
your own understanding; in all your ways acknowledge
him, and he will make your paths straight.
—Proverbs 3:5–6

All I'd ever wanted was to be a mom. I played with baby dolls from the time I was a toddler. When people would ask me what I wanted to be when I grew up, my answer was always the same—I want to be a mommy. Even at age thirteen, I'd play with Cabbage Patch Dolls and baby dolls pretending I was their mama. I also loved porcelain dolls. I had one that looked exactly like and weighed about the same as a real baby. I'd take it out in public, and people would have to look twice. I was infatuated with being a mom. I was young, and although many people criticized me for trying to conceive so soon after marriage, I didn't care.

I wanted to be a mom more than anything else. I kept track of periods and ovulation times and I read all the baby books. Within two months, I was pregnant. I was so excited! Finally, I'd have my own baby to love and be loved by. I did everything right, but it wasn't God's timing. At eleven weeks into the pregnancy, I miscarried. I stayed in bed alternating between crying and staring at a wall for days. My husband felt helpless as I slipped into despair. I didn't talk. I didn't eat. I didn't leave the house. I was lost in my own suffering. Through prayer I was able to come back to the land of the living. My husband took me on a surprise trip to a bed and breakfast, convinced me we'd try again, and this time, it would work out. We spent much time in prayer over that weekend and throughout the next weeks asking God to send us a baby.

Then one day, a younger coworker was talking about a camping trip being planned to celebrate her birthday. She mentioned a friend who wanted to go but was having trouble finding care for her four-month-old for the whole weekend. When I asked about her family, my coworker said this poor girl had been kicked out of her home because of the baby. The baby's dad was a drug addict, and she was doing whatever she could to care for this baby alone. I wanted to help this girl, so I offered to babysit during that weekend if she would entrust her child with someone she did not know.

I fell in love with Christopher the moment I laid eyes on him. He had dark skin, big brown eyes, soft curly hair, and a smile that would melt your heart. When we gave him back to his mama that Sunday afternoon, I told her we'd watch him anytime. She got tears in her eyes as she said, "Thank you so much! I haven't had any support with him, and it's been hard. My job wants me to work on the weekends, but I don't have anyone to watch him. Do you think you could? It would really help me to be able to make that extra money."

My heart ached for her and this precious baby. Without hesitation, I said yes!

Unfortunately, my husband didn't share my enthusiasm. He said weekends were our time to spend together, and if there's a baby here all the time, when would we have time for us? I urged him to recognize how much this girl and her helpless baby needed us. After reminding him that we'd been praying for a baby and that he was called into youth ministry, he agreed we could take care of the baby one weekend at a time. He also said it would definitely not be an every-weekend commitment. Little did we know our lives were about to dramatically change.

Father, I thank you that I don't know the whole plan. There are times I want to know the next steps or the future, but I understand that it would be too much for me to take. Thank you for the promise that you go before me, prepare the way, and walk beside me. You are more than enough!

CHAPTER 8

*Then I heard the voice of the Lord saying, "Whom shall I send?
And who shall go for us?" and I said, "Here I am. Send me!"*
—*Isaiah 6:8*

*Now it is required that those who have been
given a trust must prove faithful.*
—*1 Corinthians 4:2*

About a month after that first weekend with Christopher, around nine thirty one evening, there was an unexpected knock on our door. My husband went to the door to find the young mom and her baby. She had been crying. She handed the baby over and said she had just been kicked out of the place she was staying. She said she had another place she could go in two weeks but in the meantime didn't know what to do.

My husband took her hand in his, told her we were there for her, and she could stay with us. She pulled her hand away and said she just wanted to see if Christopher could stay with us. She said she could stay with friends so that she could be closer to school and work. I told her I understood; however, we both had to work the next day. I didn't see how we could possibly take him for two weeks. I asked her to stay that night, told her I would take off work the next day, and we'd work on a plan. Sobbing, she then appealed to me saying she needed a break. She wanted us to take him that night, and she'd come back tomorrow to make a plan.

My husband and I looked at each other and agreed. She thanked us and said we were the only ones who had ever been there for her in life. She kissed the baby and quickly left. I called to inform my employer I would not be in the next day and went to bed. The next morning, I tried to call her a couple of times. It kept going to voice-mail. I left a message. That afternoon when I still hadn't heard back from her and she hadn't yet shown up, I called again and left another message. I called my coworker and her friend to see if she had any other contact number or way to contact her. She didn't, but she tried to reach her as well. She, too, had to leave a message.

That night at about 10:00 p.m., my phone rang. It was a girl claiming to be a friend of the young mother. She said she was calling to let us know that the mother of the baby we had in our possession was in jail. She said the baby was brought to us because she knew she'd be caught and put in jail. I was very surprised! I asked why, what had she done? The girl explained the baby's mother was a drug dealer. She said that was what this girl was doing while Christopher was in our care. She was surprised we didn't know. I was flabbergasted! Of course I didn't know! If I would have known, I wouldn't have just let it go! I asked how long she would be in jail. I wondered if it would be two weeks. The girl responded by laughing and said, "Who knows how long she'll be in jail!"

I looked at my husband with tears streaming down my face. Now what were we supposed to do? He said we needed to figure out who Christopher's father was and go to him or to the grandparents. However, I was already way too attached and felt we should just keep him. My husband was the voice of reason though; he wasn't ours, we had no legal standing, and we couldn't just keep him.

After a good night of sleep, I knew he was right—we couldn't just keep him. We had to tell his father what was going on. We were able to locate Christopher's paternal grandparents that next afternoon. We found out that the father was a teenager as well. We sat in the grandparents' living room as Christopher's father explained that he was not ready for this responsibility, and he wanted nothing to do with the baby. Grandma and Grandpa explained that they could not take care of this baby either.

I was crying. My husband was visibly angry. So what were we supposed to do? We both had jobs. We did not have the money to take care of a baby. The father stood up, looked at us, then at Christopher and told us to take him to foster care. With that he walked out of the room. I looked at Grandma and Grandpa and asked if that was really what they wanted for their grandson—foster care. The grandma left the room. The grandpa then asked if we could just give them a few minutes.

They came back into the living room about ten minutes later and sat down. Then she said, "Look, it's not ideal, but these two are way over their heads with this baby. You obviously love Christopher and have formed a bond with him over the past couple of months. I will pay for a lawyer if you will take him in and be his foster parents. I will also pay for childcare and anything else you need until everything gets settled legally."

My husband and I talked privately, and we both very strongly felt that Christopher was the baby we'd been praying for. We both believed that this was God's leading of what we were supposed to do.

Thank you, Lord, that each of us has a different calling. I love that you call the broken and wayward to do far more than we think we can do. Then you equip us to do all you ask of us. And as if that isn't enough, then you bless us for our obedience and trust in you. You are an awesome God!

CHAPTER 9

*You armed me with strength for battle; you
humbled my adversaries before me.*
                              —*Psalm 18:39*

*But the Lord is faithful, and he will strengthen
you and protect you from the evil one.*
                              —*2 Thessalonians 3:3*

After Christopher had been with us for a while, his mom called and said she was taking him for an overnight. I did not want to let him go! I was afraid for his safety. But what could I do? We didn't have legal custody of him yet. I packed a diaper bag and prayed. She picked him up from our house about lunchtime. He was still taking his nap, and I wanted him to eat before she left. However, she insisted that they were going immediately, and she'd be able to feed him. Helplessly, I watched them walk out the door, get in the car, and drive away.

The plan was for Christopher to be returned to us at eight the next evening. At 8:20 p.m., there was no sign of her. I finally got through to her by phone at 8:40 p.m. She had all kinds of excuses saying she wouldn't be able to meet me but could I pick him up. She gave me directions to a run-down trailer park. The trailer door was opened by a drunk man in his forties. When the door opened, smoke came out. What I saw as I stepped inside made my stomach sick and my head spin. There was another man in his forties, a man in his twenties, an older teenage boy, a younger teenage girl, Christopher, and his mom. She and the other teen girl were dressed very provocatively. She was obviously drunk or high. When Christopher saw me, he dropped his bottle of Kool-Aid and ran to me. He was in the same clothes as the day before, wearing a completely full and soaked diaper, was dirty, and he smelled horrible. It was as if he hadn't been watched at all during the thirty-three hours since he'd left my care. He and I clung to each other.

I asked her how she could let this happen to him. Tears were streaming down my face. She just laughed and said, "He's fine."

I cried all the way home. After I had bathed Christopher, put him in pajamas, fed him, and rocked him with a bottle, I talked to my husband. I knew we needed some sort of emergency help so that she could not take him out of our home again. We decided to call the lawyer in the morning and figure out how to proceed. I was determined not to let this happen again!

By the end of that week, we were in front of a judge for an emergency hearing. An ex parte order was signed giving us temporary sole physical custody. It also stated that his biological mom was only able to see Christopher in a supervised setting. She found out about it six days later when she asked for a visit with Christopher. It was a rough interaction!

Two months later, we had court. She came into court with written statements from her roommate and three children who were under the age of eight. The judge wouldn't even look at them. Her behavior was out of control in the courtroom. She made several outbursts, interrupted our lawyer, interrupted the judge, and yelled at us. She dug herself into a hole, and the more she said, the deeper that hole got. She walked into court that day expecting to get Christopher back. In the end, what she got was a stern lecture from the judge. He told her she had to do four things in order to get him back—find a respectable job, find an apartment, get a car, and take responsibility for what she has and has not done. Because we were petitioning the court for permanent custody, the judge also ordered custody evaluations for all four of us as well as chemical dependency and random UAs (urine drug tests) for both mom and dad. Christopher's dad hadn't even shown up that day!

In addition to the custody hearing, Christopher's mom was going through a presentence investigation because she had pleaded guilty to twelve felony counts for possession and intent to sell illegal drugs. She received three years' probation, a $300 fine, and one hundred hours of community service. My husband and I went through the evaluations easily. It was evident that we had a very close bond with Christopher, and unfortunately, Mom did not. The subsequent home visits also went very well for us.

During this time, his dad had started to see Christopher every other weekend, and they had formed a bond as well. At this point, it was April 1, 1999, two years since Christopher came to live with us. This was the day that all paperwork would be signed giving us permanent custody of Christopher; he would be our adopted son! Mom had lost all her rights, and Dad was in full support of us.

There was a big party to celebrate planned for that night. We were so excited as we walked into court that day! So what happened next stunned us to the core. Dad and his mother (grandma) walked into court with a lawyer. He had decided he couldn't go through with giving up his rights, and he wanted his son back. He was now fighting us for custody! The anger I felt toward Christopher's dad was immense as was the sadness. More evaluations were ordered, and the next court date was set for August 26, 1999. That date brought only one thing—more waiting. The judge said we'd need to go to trial.

On November 29, 1999, Christopher's dad was awarded custody back. December would be a transition month, and starting in January, Christopher would live with his dad and visit us every other weekend. It was a huge loss, but it was also a time of leaning into God. My healer, defender, daddy and friend showed himself mightily throughout this time. He made it clear that I had done exactly what he asked of me. He held me up and set me back on my feet again. I knew without a doubt Christopher would be okay and that I had fulfilled my role in his life!

As I write this book, Christopher is a healthy, happy, well-adjusted adult. He is in a loving, healthy relationship. He is an amazing dad to two beautiful children. He and his mom have a great relationship. (Following treatment, Christopher's mom was able to turn her life around. She is a follower of Jesus, and it shows!) Christopher has a great job. Most importantly, he has a relationship with Jesus Christ. I thank God for the time I had with him when he was young and that we have a relationship to this day! He has been one of the greatest blessings of my life!

Father, thank you for the blessing of Christopher. Thank you for all I learned through this experience. I pray you will help me and those reading this story to trust in all you have for each of us.

CHAPTER 10

For you created my inmost being; you knit me together in my mother's womb. I praise you because I am fearfully and wonderfully made.
—*Psalm 139:13–14*

Your word is a lamp for my feet, a light unto my path.
—*Psalm 119:105*

During the years with Christopher, I learned that infertility would be a part of my story. Ovulation kits, taking temperatures, drugs with hormones, injections, inseminations, in vitro…these are the words that come to rule your days when you go through infertility, along with heartbreak, anger, frustration, and sadness.

For this chapter, I will be sharing with you excerpts from the journal I wrote during my four years of infertility:

> *I feel so empty inside. My tears keep flowing and I cannot stop. The doctor looked at all the tests we did and said I looked healthy but my body just isn't doing what it is supposed to. I don't seem to be ovulating and his sperm count is really low. It's been a year of trying; six months of which has been on fertility drugs. I'm not sure I can take much more.*
>
> *We just held each other last night and spent hours in prayer. We only want to do what God wants for us. Because of God's goodness I've been losing some of the sadness every day.*

In today's mail was all the paperwork from the reproductive endocrinologist. It's pretty scary! I always thought having a baby was the most natural thing in the world but not this way! In Vitro Fertilization sounds like some sort of alien abduction!

There was a baby dedication at church this morning. I had to leave the sanctuary. God, why?

I talked with a woman named Katherine today. She is the leader of the support group we are going to attend. It was wonderful to talk to a godly woman who knows exactly what I'm going through! No one knows until they are in these shoes. The anger this provokes is unbelievable! We talked about how angry we get at pregnant women and how jealousy can come in and steal our joy; we talked about women and men who don't realize how wonderful a gift from God their kids are and they either treat them horribly or have abortions and how irate that makes us. She said something to me though that really made me think…

"They don't know what an incredible gift from God they have. And we don't know what they have or what they may be going through. BUT…isn't it great that because we are experiencing this we will realize what a glorious gift our children are when we do have them!"

She also helped me with what to say to those who tell me to Just Relax; Stop Thinking About It. People who say that have no idea what I'm going through. They don't know what to say so they are doing the best they can. I need to take it for what it is…someone trying to help. It was so wonderful to have my feelings validated today.

Just because I have this issue does not mean I don't trust God. It just means that the struggle God has allowed us to go through (before he blesses us with a child) will give me what I need to be a great mom. He has me in the palm of His hand. He is in control and I am not.

I'm learning more and more about God through this process. I'm actually coming to a point where I'm thankful for infertility because of how much closer to God it has brought me. I'm realizing that just because I want it, I prayed for it, and I believe it doesn't mean it will happen. It has to be His will and His timing. I have to trust Him in the process. Easier said than done but I'm trying.

We've made a very difficult decision. We're going to stop going to doctors and take a year off. It's time to think about something else. We're going to concentrate on our marriage. The top infertility specialist in Minnesota told us that we have a 0% chance of conceiving.

Two and a half years after that entry came this entry:

You're here!! Praise God!! I don't think I've ever been this happy!! I went to the doctor today because every time I eat I get an upset stomach. When I called the nurseline to make the appointment, the nurse was positive I was pregnant. I took a urine test and then met with the doctor. She said I seemed pretty healthy. She asked how I'd feel if the test was positive. I said I'd be really, really happy but also scared because of the miscarriage but I really doubted it would be positive anyway. She left and when she returned I said, "so, I'm sure it was negative. Now what."

She smiled and said, "Actually, it was positive."

I didn't believe her until I saw the printout. She sent me directly up to the OB department to get an ultrasound to see how far along I was. When I got to the desk in that department and started to say the words "I'm pregnant" I lost it. I was hysterical. She came around the desk and hugged me. I then turned to see my husband, who was standing there with tears in his eyes and I confirmed that yes, we were going to have a baby.

God, children are such a blessing! I lift up those who want so badly to become parents and are having trouble conceiving. I know the pain that causes. I ask that you comfort, protect, and walk beside these people. Lord, you are a loving God who knows our innermost desires. The most important thing I learned from infertility is that YOU *are enough—*YOU *are sufficient. If you never did another thing, I would have enough to be thankful for eternity. Thank you for the cross, thank you that Jesus rose again, and thank you that you are preparing a place for us!*

CHAPTER 11

*Now the L*ORD *was gracious to Sarah as he had said, and
the L*ORD *did for Sarah what he had promised.*
—Genesis 21:1

*The name Josiah in the Bible means "Healed of
the Lord" or "The Lord will support."*

In early 2000, at 7:19 p.m., my sweet baby boy was born. He had
so much skin and so little body that when they held him up for
me to see, all I could think of were the wrinkly dogs thus the
nickname Wrinkles was also born.

In the hospital, he slept through the night both nights. I thought,
This is going to be the easiest baby ever! On the third night, we were
home, and boy did I get a wake-up call! At 4:00 a.m., we hadn't gone
to bed yet, Josiah and I were crying uncontrollably, and Daddy was
beside himself. I even called the hospital maternity ward and asked
if we could come back. Their response? "Give him a pacifier!" I did,
and everyone went to sleep. I didn't want him to have a pacifier (new
mom mistake number one), but it definitely solved the problem!

After that, I did have a very easy baby. He talked and walked
super early. He was very obedient. He was a huge blessing! During
the first couple of years of Josiah's life, we saw Christopher every
other weekend. Time with him started to wane after that, but we still
saw him as often as possible. As far as we were concerned, he'll always
be our first child, and Josiah knew him as his big brother.

Josiah's teen years were almost as easy as the younger years. He
was always so obedient, a huge help with his brothers, and he was
in the National Honor Society, and speech, drama, and art club.

He started college wanting to be a high school history teacher and graduated with a degree in psychology. During his freshman year, he met Clara, one of the loveliest girls I've ever met. They're now college graduates working in their respective fields of study and building a life together.

About a year later, he came to me with the admission that he didn't believe in God or the Bible anymore and would never attend church again. He was very worried that I would be disappointed in him. I told him my love for him is unconditional as is God's. I told him that because he had asked Jesus to be his Savior at one point in his life, I believed he would go to heaven because you cannot lose your salvation. I told him no matter what happens in life, he will always have me by his side. I assured him I would be praying for God to draw him back and that whenever he was ready, God would be there with open arms.

So he's currently trying to make it in the world without leaning into Jesus and that makes life harder than it has to be. However, we are very close, and I continue to pray and have faith that he will return to Christian beliefs someday. After all, the Bible says in Proverbs 22:6, *"Train up a child in the way he should go; and when he is old he will not depart from it."*

Thank you, Lord, for the gift of Josiah. I have been abundantly blessed by his life.

CHAPTER 12

*It may be that the Lord will look upon my misery and restore
to me his covenant blessing instead of his curse today.*
—2 Samuel 16:12

The meaning of Elijah in the Bible is "Yahweh is my God."

After being told by a top infertility specialist that I had zero chance of conceiving a child, I truly felt that Josiah was my miracle baby. I was very much under the impression that he would be my only biological child. So when I started having pregnancy symptoms about a year after he was born, I thought I just had the flu. However, it seemed there would be another miracle to come!

In late 2002, I delivered (too quickly for the doctor to even get in the room) another baby boy with the most beautiful big blue eyes. Eli was the sweetest baby. I could lay him down anywhere, and as long as he had his special blankie, he would easily go to sleep.

Unfortunately, we had to overcome many obstacles in his first year. He was tongue-tied (his tongue was attached to the bottom of his mouth) which made it difficult for him to nurse. At four months old, we found out he was allergic to both my milk and regular formula. The most challenging of all was I had severe postpartum depression bordering on psychosis. This depression was unlike anything I had previously experienced. It wasn't that I didn't love my baby. It was that I loved him so much that I thought he deserved a better mom than me.

One example of the extreme that I was willing to go to, to "save" him from me was the day I left him at a large store. Although I don't remember all the details, I'll share what I do recall. I fed him, wrote a note explaining myself, tucked it in his car seat, and left him in the store bathroom. Josiah was with me, and as we left the bathroom, my always compliant little boy stopped. He refused to move until I went back for Eli. He saved us that day. I knew I needed help for what was going on with me.

Eli turned out to be the funniest, happiest little boy. He loved all sports, especially basketball. He easily made friends, and there were boys staying at our house frequently throughout his childhood. As a teenager, he made some poor choices, and he and I drifted apart. We argued often, and it was a rough period. However, in time, he matured, and I recognized the places where I fell short.

We are now very close. He is in a good relationship with a lovely girl. They are both maturing in their adulthood, and it is exciting (and sometimes challenging) to see them grow. I'm so proud to be his mom and grateful I received this second miracle!

Thank you, Lord, for the gift of Eli! Thank you for delivering me through the struggle of postpartum depression. Help those women who are going through this to recognize that you are with them. Lead them to healing.

CHAPTER 13

*Then your light will break forth like the dawn, and your
healing will quickly appear; then your righteousness will go
before you, and the glory of the Lord will be your rear guide.*
—Isaiah 58:8

The meaning of Micah in the Bible is "Who is like God."

Due to the postpartum depression after delivering Eli, I chose
to get a birth control implant. My body, however, rejected
it. I ended up with a high fever and intense pain which
brought me to the emergency room. There I was told the implant
had gotten infected and needed to come out. I was in the hospital
overnight and then sent home to heal.

About ten months later in late 2004, Micah entered the world.
He was gorgeous! He was a welcome addition to our family. From the
beginning, he was a child of extremes—extremely happy, extremely
upset, extremely funny, extremely loving, extremely naughty, etc.

While Josiah was artsy, Eli loved all sports. Micah was a com-
bination of both. He was in an art club and played lots of sports,
baseball being his favorite. School was always difficult for him. Life
in general sometimes seemed challenging as well. He was often very
angry and expressed it by kicking in doors, throwing objects, hitting
his fists and head into the walls, and yelling. I couldn't understand
why he was so angry.

At thirteen he went to live at a residential treatment facility for
youth ages eighteen to twenty who were dealing with mental health
concerns. It was an amazing transformation. In the eight months he
was there, he learned why he was so angry and how to cope with life's

challenges. While going through this process was one of the more difficult things either of us have ever dealt with, it was worth it.

At sixteen we almost lost him. He was involved in a near fatal car accident with friends. He had to have a blood transfusion, had a punctured lung, a broken rib, a torn spleen, and a severe road rash. He also had four plates and twenty screws inserted to repair a broken scapula. I couldn't and can't imagine my life without him. As tough as some things have been, I would do it all over again for him.

Micah still struggles with mental health concerns. However, he is willing to put effort into everything he does. He's kept up with going to church, getting professional help when needed, and going to work. It has not been an easy road for him. I pray every day that he will learn to love himself as much as I love him and that he will learn to see himself through God's eyes.

Thank you, Lord, for the gift of Micah. Thank you for saving him. I know you have a great purpose for his life. I pray for the parents that struggle through how to parent a child with mental health struggles. It is a difficult journey; however, you are always there. Help me and these other parents to give their children over to you, to know you are in control, and to trust in the process.

CHAPTER 14

*Do not conform to the pattern of this world, but be transformed
by the renewing of your mind. Then you will be able to test and
approve what God's will is—his good, pleasing, and perfect will.*
—Romans 12:2

*Trust in him at all times, oh you people; pour out
your hearts to him, for God is our refuge.*
—Psalm 62:8

By the time Micah was two years old, my marriage was crumbling. There had been many events that led up to the day I packed my husband's bag, changed the locks, and told him he needed to leave. For many years I placed all of the blame on him. However, as I've grown and matured, I see how I contributed to the difficulties in our marriage.

Even before we even got married, I knew our relationship wasn't what I wanted and sensed something was wrong. Looking back, I might not have attempted suicide shortly after we were engaged if everything was right. There was nobody to blame; it just was what it was.

When I was pregnant with Josiah, I discovered his addiction to pornography. Although it had been going on long before we were a couple, I definitely took it personally. He tried to stop by joining a Christian men's group called Every Man's Battle. I even spoke to other women going through the same thing in an attempt to heal myself of everything that was a part of the addiction. I see now I could never have "healed myself." Only God has the power to heal.

Another issue in our marriage was that I was very controlling. After much therapy, I can now admit what I denied at that time.

36

I've learned that I was (and still am to a point) controlling because it helped calm my anxiety. I've been through so much trauma in life that my brain tricked me into believing the more I could control, the less hurt I would get. That was not true!

His difficulty keeping a job resulted in stressful financial issues. When we separated, I was working three jobs in order to support us, and I brought the boys with me to two of those jobs.

His frustration with life not going how he wanted got the better of him many times. Frustration turned to anger that would get out of control. He would throw and break things, yell, bang his head on the walls, push me against a wall, and then punch the wall close to my head. It became a scary place to exist. I kept the peace as much as I could because I didn't want my kids to know what was happening. I was miserable, but in my mind, a "good Christian girl" didn't get a divorce.

Back when I was thirteen and my mom filed for divorce (even though he was the one that left), we were going to a church that forbade divorce. When the pastor heard mom had filed for divorce, he told her that good Christian women don't divorce; therefore, she was no longer welcome in the church. He told her that I could still come to youth events, but she was not welcome. I did not continue at the church, and his words stuck with me.

One particular morning when my husband and I were arguing, Micah got in the middle. He picked Micah up by the arm and threw him out of the way. Thankfully he landed safely on the couch, but he could've been seriously hurt. That was the day I told him he needed to leave. I was not going to allow our toxic relationship to spill over and hurt my boys.

Father, I pray for every marriage bond and for the children that are brought into these relationships. We are a broken people, and we do hurtful things. We make mistakes and sin every day. The sanctity of marriage in our country has been compromised in many cases, sin abounds, and children are caught in the middle. I pray for healing for our collective hearts and a desire so strong it cannot be overcome to seek you in all circumstances. Nothing is impossible when you are in it!

CHAPTER 15

*So the king gave the order, and they brought Daniel and
they threw him into the lions' den. The king said to Daniel,
"May your God who you serve continually, save you."*
                                                    —*Daniel 6:16*

They draw near to the pit, and their life to the messengers of death.
                                                    —*Job 33:22*

Like I said earlier after the kidnapping, I blocked all of my father's abuse from my memory. In 2008 I was actively seeking therapy due to the separation from my husband. It quickly evolved to talking about my childhood. I wanted to get to the root of my depression and anxiety, so I could give it all to God and move forward. Unfortunately, it would not be that easy.

I was undergoing deep psychological treatment, and the memories of childhood abuse all came crashing back. The psychologist then diagnosed me with PTSD. It was all so overwhelming! As an adult looking back on the abuse, I felt as though all I was worth to my father was to be his sex toy. I felt dirty, unloved, and worthless.

Within a couple of months of memories resurfacing, my papa died. He was the one man in my life who had never hurt me. I had him on a pedestal because he seemed like the perfect husband and father. Papa taught me the importance of quiet and of listening for the voice of God. He and Granny had been married for fifty-two years. I watched her fall apart. He had taken care of all the finances, the maintenance, the cars, etc. I remember her sitting at the kitchen table looking at the checkbook and saying over and over again, "I don't know how to write a check or pay a bill." Since I was giving the eulogy at his funeral, I channeled my initial grief into preparing what I would say.

By this time, my marriage was over. He had moved to an apartment, and I was grieving the loss of what could've been. All of this proved to be more than my brain could handle, and one day, it just shut down. I remember it being a sunny August day and getting the boys ready to go to the pool.

I don't remember much that took place over the next thirty hours until I opened my eyes and immediately felt fear. *What have I done!?* I thought. *I have to hide their bodies!* The thoughts running through my head were of their little lifeless bodies lying on the floor in the living room. I knew there was blood from where I'd stabbed them the night before. I couldn't believe what I had done. What was wrong with me? Why couldn't I ever get it together?

I threw the blankets off and ran into the living room. They weren't there! *Did someone already find them? Did I already bury them and clean up the blood? Okay, calm down. Maybe it was all a horrible dream and they are sleeping in their beds.* I ran to their bedroom. Beds were unmade, but there were no little boys sleeping. Then I ran outside screaming their names. I was desperate to find them alive. However, I knew in my heart that I'd stabbed them with a knife in the living room the night before. *Why don't I remember burying them? And all that blood…when did I clean that up?*

My next stop was the kitchen cupboard and then the bathroom where I kept all of the medications. I grabbed every single pill I could find because I knew I couldn't go to jail. I wanted to join my babies in heaven. I sat down in my bed with a big glass of water and dumped out every pill.

The phone ringing brought me momentarily out of the fog I was in. It was my sister. I told her what I had done, and she said she'd send help. I told her I'd be dead by then and hung up. Not long after that brief conversation, my best friend and an ambulance arrived, and I was taken to the hospital. I was adamant that they had to find out what I had done with the boys. They kept telling me they were alive, safe, and happy with their dad, but I didn't believe them. When they'd tell me I didn't harm them, I'd yell at them to stop lying.

After three days in the hospital, no one had been able to convince me that my boys were alive. They finally allowed me to talk with them on the phone. I had to promise not to ask the boys questions about that morning or talk to them about being stabbed. The doctors and my family were concerned I would scare them.

When I heard their voices, it was as if a switch turned on inside of me. They were their usual wonderful little boy selves. They wondered where I was and when I was coming home. They said Daddy, Nana, Laura, and Heather were taking good care of them, but they missed me. I was overcome with gratitude! I cannot describe what it felt like to hear their voices after thinking they had been dead for the last three days.

Now I had a mission. I had to get well. I had to be back with my boys. The moment I heard their voices, the real work of healing began. After working hard for two days, I asked if there was any way I could see my boys. My doctor arranged for a pass permitting me to be in my sister's care and go to the park across the street from the hospital. There we met my husband, the boys, my friends, and their kids. It was an amazing thing to actually see them, hug them, and talk to them. It was healing to hear them laugh and play! I felt at that moment that I could conquer the whole world.

I went back to the hospital for two more days. It was decided that I would be released on the seventh day on the condition that I commit to outpatient DBT treatment, treatment for my eating disorder, and supervised visits with my children for the next twelve weeks. Regarding the supervised visits, it was difficult and humbling to find myself in the same position as Christopher's mom had been.

Dear Lord, I have felt so much comfort and compassion from you over the years. What I have not felt is condemnation. You are always faithful, always merciful, and always full of grace. I know I am not alone in what I have experienced. I know you are just as available to others as you are to me. Thank you for always being present. You are mighty to save, an ever-present help in times of need, and a strong tower of refuge.

CHAPTER 16

Then many will give thanks on our behalf for the gracious
favor granted us in answer to the prayers of many.
—*2 Corinthians 1:11*

For I know the plans I have for you, says the Lord. Plans to prosper
you and not to harm you. Plans to give you a hope and a future.
—*Jeremiah 29:11*

A year later in August of 2009, I moved back to my hometown. My husband and I were on again, off again in our relationship. It still didn't feel right to get a divorce, we were getting along pretty well, and I was undecided about what to do with the boys. I didn't want to uproot their whole life and their dad wanted them to start school in Burnsville, so I agreed to move without them. I worked all day and then went to see them for a few hours after work, helped put them to bed, and then drove home. I was exhausted, the body aches I'd been feeling for quite a while were getting worse, and the depression came back.

One day while I was driving on a highway, all I could think about was how easy it would be to accelerate and let the car crash into the back of a semi. I called my sister who was my number one on-call crisis person and told her what I was thinking.

"You need to find a church in your town!" She said, "I want you to turn the car around, go home, and I'll try to find a pastor who can talk and pray with you today." I did what she asked.

She proceeded to go online looking for churches in my area. Finding two that she thought would be great matches, she wrote down the contact information and called the first. Somehow, she dialed the number for the second instead. So when the receptionist answered, my sister was confused but quickly realized her mistake. She asked for a pastor and was transferred to Pastor Dan. Explaining that her sister recently moved to town and was struggling with depression, she asked if he'd be available to pray with her sister that day. He told her he was on his way out the door, but he'd see if the receptionist could find an available elder.

I'm sure you've heard the phrase "coincidences are God's way of remaining anonymous." That's exactly what happened next! While my sister was calling me back, Pastor Dan was getting a call. The person he had been out the door to see needed to cancel. He suddenly had an open two-hour time slot. He and I met at a coffee shop, talked, and prayed.

I immediately felt loved by him. He was kind, compassionate, and godly. We both sensed God had led me to him and to his church. There was a Bible study starting that night! Describing the woman hosting as a wonderful woman, he assured me I would be welcomed with open arms. He asked me to promise that I would go, but I didn't think I could just walk up to some stranger's house and introduce myself. He offered to personally drive me there and walk up to the door with me. The Bible study was called Breaking Free, and he fully believed it was where God wanted me to be. I thanked him and promised I would go.

That night, I walked up to the door of the woman who became a great mentor in my life. She prays for me and with me, she is and has been a constant in my life, and has helped me through many of life's challenges. I don't know what I would've done without her! Plus, many of the other women in that room have remained close as well. I'm so glad God made my sister dial the wrong number that day!

Thank you for "coincidences." Thank you for lining up exactly what I needed in this time of great despair. God, I pray for those who are in a dark pit. I pray that you would open their eyes to see you and to see how you are right there—carrying them, preparing the path for them, and doing far more than they can ever think or imagine.

CHAPTER 17

*Then Hannah prayed and said, "My heart rejoices in the
Lord; in the Lord my horn is lifted high. My mouth boasts
over my enemies, for I delight in your deliverance."*
—1 Samuel 2:1

In September 2009, the boys, their dad, and I went to an apple orchard for the day. I was still struggling with whether I should file for divorce or not. I asked him to move in with me and give our marriage another shot. He then informed me that he had fallen in love with someone else, filed for divorce, and wanted me to sign the papers. He also dropped the bomb that he wanted custody of the boys.

I asked everyone I knew to pray for the situation. I begged God to intervene so that I could have my boys living with me. The court had assigned a guardian ad litem to conduct home visits with us at our separate homes. She then would make a recommendation regarding who should have custody. When I received her report in the mail, I was stunned! He had been using my mental health struggles against me—giving her his version of the truth. Her report stated that he didn't feel I could safely parent alone. Even though she felt the boys and I had a stronger bond, she was recommending he get custody.

My days were filled with continued prayer and seeking God. I leaned into him with everything I had. The boys and I were seeing each other on weekends, and they were asking to live with me. They

43

were telling me that things weren't good between them and their dad's new girlfriend. I kept telling them that everything would work out in the end; we just needed to trust that God had a plan. He definitely did!

Christmas 2009 came and the boys were to spend all of Christmas break with me. The day before they were to go back to their dad, he called me. He said he had changed his mind, he couldn't handle taking care of them, and I could have them. The boys and I were thrilled! I enrolled them in school and filed all the paperwork with the court to make it official. This was just one of the many ways in which God has walked beside us in our life. At that time, I also made a decision that I would focus the next few years on my mental health and on raising my boys—no dating, no men!

God, I thank you so much for being my strong tower of refuge! No matter how difficult life gets, I know I have you. I also know that you are there for those reading these words. I pray that whatever is going on in their life, they will feel your amazing presence, comfort, and peace.

CHAPTER 18

For I know the plans I have for you, declares the Lord, plans to prosper
you and not to harm you, plans to give you a hope and a future.
                                                            —Jeremiah 29:11

Then you will call on me and come and pray to me,
and I will listen to you. You will seek me and find
me when you seek me with all your heart.
                                                    —Jeremiah 29:12–13

Four years later, I found myself being pursued by a man who would turn my world on end. He had been married for twenty-five years. They had so much in common, and he thought it was a good marriage. Then one day, she announced she was leaving him to be with a woman. He was devastated!

After eight months of living alone, he knew he didn't want to be single forever. There was a woman he would talk to on the phone. She lived an hour away. She was his insurance agent. He liked the way she sounded on the phone, the way she laughed, the way she listened to him, and the way she seemed to understand him in a way that no one else could.

One day he asked her if they could go out for coffee sometime. She said no. He started sending her emails with jokes to make her laugh. He'd call with a made-up insurance question just so he had an excuse to talk to her. Her voice made him happy where he hadn't felt happy for a long time. After the fourth time she rejected his request for a date, he thought maybe he should give up. But then three days later, an email appeared on his screen:

> I'm sending this from my personal email because I'm thinking it would be frowned upon to hit on the clients. I'm interested in drinks or dinner. If you'd like to call me tonight (or another night), here's my phone number.

He was shocked and excited. That night, he called her, and they talked for three hours. She was all the things he was looking for in a woman. There was just one issue—he was eighteen years older than her. Was there even a chance for them?

*****

The first time he asked me to dinner, my initial reaction was "Eww! He is way too old!" However, every time I talked to him, those thoughts lessened. When he asked me the fourth time, something prompted me to give him a chance. My thought was *Fine, one date. It'll feel like I'm dating an old man, and that will be the end of that!*

We met at a restaurant. He was already seated when I came in. As I walked up to the table, he rose from his seat, smiled, and hugged me. We had spent no less than ten hours on the phone together since my initial yes, and I was excited to talk with him. As I slid into my seat in the booth, he slid in next to me.

Smiling nervously, I asked what he was doing. He told me he was just so excited that this was finally happening, and he wanted to be close to me. His excitement was catchy, and I had never before met a man like him. I looked at my menu as he looked at me and told me how pretty my hair was, how pretty I was. Once I decided what to eat, I set the menu down and turned toward him. I insisted he go sit on the other side of the booth. His lip actually started pouting as he asked why.

Laughter spilled out of me as I told him I needed to be able to look at him for a while. I couldn't believe how young he looked for his age! He asked if I would hold his hand, and I told him I would be happy to. We talked and talked. The more I talked to him, looked at him, felt his thumb brush over my hand, the more I liked him. This was not going as I had planned. An hour after our meal ended, he asked if I'd like to go to a movie. Neither of us were ready for the night to end.

As we walked to the car, he looked down and asked if I always wore thongs. *What?!* He had been so thoughtful and gentlemanly all through dinner. I couldn't believe he had asked me this!

Completely innocent, he said, "You know, your shoes. They're thongs." I was roaring with laughter! I had found something that definitely showed our age difference.

Once I could control my laughter, I told him, "No, I don't always wear thongs, and the things on my feet are no longer called thongs. They are called flip flops. Thongs are now what we call underwear with no cheeks."

Seeing his mistake, he, too, started laughing. That will forever be our joke!

At the movie, we held hands, and emotions started stirring inside me. I was shocked that this had gone so well. After the movie, we were standing by his car, he put his hand on my face, and said he was going to kiss me. I couldn't move or speak. I just nodded yes. The next six years of my life would bring all kinds of twists and turns.

Mike not only loved me but he loved my boys as well. He took them rock climbing, hunting, flying, fishing, to do archery, snow-mobiling, four wheeling, and much more. He'd bring me shopping and cause a stir in the store as he whooped and hollered as if he was at a fashion show, and I was the star. I had never felt so good about myself as I did when I was with him.

He had two grown boys that I very much enjoyed spending time with. The second year we were together, we took a big family vacation to Florida. There were nine of us. We went to the Disney parks and two beaches. One of his sons proposed to his girlfriend while we were there. It was magical!

It wasn't always so magical though. He had a difficult time telling me he loved me and said he'd never get married again. This was difficult for me because I didn't want to be a "girlfriend" for the rest of my life. I wondered if we would even be together for the rest of our lives if he couldn't commit. There were other issues as well. One was that we wanted very different things for the retirement years of our lives. Another issue was that I was diagnosed with fibromyalgia and chronic fatigue syndrome. And of course, the mental health issues were still there.

He was very much a "mind over matter" kind of person. He felt I should be able to fight through the pain and fatigue, choose to be happy, and then life would be grand. I wish it were that easy! In 2016, I had a major depressive episode. My therapist called Mike to tell him I should go to the hospital and asked if he could bring me. He said he would bring me. However, at the hospital, he told me that I needed to work through this and let him know when I was ready to choose happiness. When I got out of the hospital, I called him and told him everything was good. I had made a promise to myself to never again speak to him about my mental health.

More and more I sensed him pulling away from me. He was making comments that gave me the distinct impression that it was his intention to break off our relationship the next time he saw me. I wrote him a letter begging him not to leave me, professing my undying love for him, and promising that I would be strong and choose happiness from now on. He read the letter, cried, admitted that it was his intention to break off our relationship, but he would give it another chance. In hindsight, I see now I was so desperate to be loved that I was willing to deny my deepest emotions and move through life pretending to be someone I was not.

Then in December of 2016, life took another turn.

Heavenly Father, thank you for giving my boys this experience of a hands-on dad in their life. Thank you for giving me this better-than-I-had-previously-known example of how a man should treat a woman.

Forgive me for the decisions I made that went against you during this time. I lift up single moms who feel lonely and scared and just want companionship. I lift up marriages that are in trouble. Help each person look to you rather than the world to meet their needs.

CHAPTER 19

He will wipe every tear from their eyes. There will be no more death or mourning or crying or pain. For the old order of things has passed away.
—Revelation 21:4

Do not be afraid of what you are about to suffer… Be faithful, even to the point of death, and I will give you life as your victor's crown.
—Revelation 2:10

I received a call at work from Mike's sister informing me that he was in the hospital. He had woken up at 4:00 a.m. with horrible abdominal pain. Of course, his attitude was "just push through it," so he took a shower and got ready for work. However, on the way to work, the pain was so excruciating that he could no longer ignore it. He drove himself to the hospital, walked in, and collapsed, unconscious at the emergency room desk.

Following scans and tests, he was diagnosed with pancreatitis. He was in the hospital for a few days, then released. Follow-up doctor appointments and scans were scheduled for January and February. At the January appointment, they saw lesions on his pancreas and liver that had grown since the scans done in December. In February, they had further progressed in size and the dreaded word *cancer* was put out as a possibility. He then went in for further testing, and we awaited results.

In mid-February we, along with his son and daughter-in-law, went to the Canada border for a snowmobiling trip. While we were there, he got the phone call; the lesions were pancreatic cancer that had metastasized to the liver. Mike told me the diagnosis very matter-of-fact, said we weren't going to cry about it, he'd get treatment and be fine, and we got back on the trails. My tears froze to my face as we continued along.

By April we had been told he had only six months to live. He had been through a few rounds of chemo and found a world-renowned surgeon in California who was willing to operate. The day we arrived, we met with the surgeon and his medical team. Mike was also able to accomplish all of his pre-surgery requirements. We then had three days to explore the city before his day of surgery.

The first day he had the opportunity to fulfill one of his dreams. He drove a race car around a race track—and he definitely did not go slow. The second day we went to a beautiful garden where there were peacocks roaming everywhere, and the house where the TV show *Fantasy Island* was filmed was on the grounds. He was too weak to walk, so I pushed him in a wheelchair throughout the park. The third day we went to a little nearby town where we browsed the shops, had a wonderful lunch, and watched a movie.

On surgery day, we had to be at the hospital quite early. Mike's sons had decided at the last minute to fly out for the day. He was in surgery for many hours. When the surgeon was ready, he called us into a room to explain his findings. He said the tumor on the liver was the size of a cantaloupe and was successfully removed. The tumor on the pancreas was also removed, but they had to remove part of the spleen as well. When they opened him up, they found around eighty other tumors varying in size on and around the liver. The surgeon felt he removed them all but cautioned that they could return, and there could've been microscopic tumors that were missed. Due to travel restrictions, we remained in California a few more days before he was able to fly home.

At his one month checkup, he did a PET scan to see how things looked after surgery. What they found was devastating. He now had hundreds of tumors throughout his abdominal area, liver, and pancreas. Although they did not do a brain scan, the doctor believed the cancer had most likely spread to the brain as well. This was the end of June, and the doctor was giving him two months at the most to live.

At the end of July, we went with friends to Canada. He wanted this one last trip, so we all agreed we'd be there for him. There were many of us, so we rented two houseboats and went out to a deserted part of the lake where there was an island to dock. That's where we stayed for a few days. We had little boats with us, so we'd go out on the lake and fish. We played cards, ate a lot of good food, sat around a bonfire at night, and enjoyed the summer warmth. At first Mike was doing well, but then he started laying around, taking naps, and not participating. This was not like him at all. Though there was much laughter on that island, I often found myself sitting alone and crying. The man I loved was going to die soon. He was in an extreme amount of pain on the car ride home. He curled up in a fetal position with his head on my lap and suffered throughout the long six-hour drive.

Two weeks later, he was in the hospital again. Fluid had been collecting in his abdomen requiring the insertion of a tube that drained almost three liters. The doctor said this was a sign that organs were shutting down, and we might want to think about hospice. Mike declined, insisting he would bounce back. His sister and I urged him to quit his job. He agreed that the three of us would meet with his boss. However, when we got there, we realized he was still very much in denial. His sister and I sat in amazement as he told his boss he was going to have to start working part time, he'd do that for a couple of months, and then he'd be back to full time. When he left the room, we informed his boss that would not be the case.

By the middle of August, he was extremely weak. He reluctantly agreed to my calling hospice. I became his around-the-clock nurse, giving him pain and nausea medications as needed. People came daily to say their goodbyes. And then early one morning, he coughed up blood, his breathing became labored, and he slipped away. I was frozen in place as I sat beside him and held his hand until the very last minute when his body was removed from the home.

Funeral arrangements were made, picture boards were put together, and on a beautiful fall day, we all said our goodbyes to Mike. It was a meaningful service celebrating his life. I walked alongside the casket as he was brought to the hearse. Because he was being cremated and there would not be a graveside service, this would be my final goodbye. Before closing the doors to the hearse, all five "sons" and I were given heart stickers. One by one we put our stickers on the back of the casket forming a cross. I was last to place my heart sticker. I then pressed my forehead against the cross we had created and released him to Jesus knowing I would see him again one day in heaven. It was a very intimate moment that I will always treasure.

God, as I reflect on this time in my life, I realize how much I learned and have been able to use for my good and for your glory. You leave nothing wasted! My heart aches for those who are currently mourning the loss of a loved one. May they seek you first and foremost. I pray they will sense your amazing comfort and realize the grief won't always be this painful.

CHAPTER 20

*But we also glory in our sufferings, because we know that suffering
produces perseverance; perseverance, character; and character, hope.*
—Romans 5:3–4

*Trust in the Lord with all your heart and lean not on
your own understanding; in all your ways submit to
him, and he will make your paths straight.*
—Proverbs 3:5–6

The next year brought many challenges as I tried to learn to live without Mike. This was the year that Micah went to the residential treatment facility, I was hospitalized twice for suicidal thoughts, and in May of 2018, I was fired from my job. By this point, I was having so many mental and physical health issues that I just couldn't hold down a job. So I filed for disability.

In June, Josiah graduated from high school, and we had a big party for him. A few of Mike's friends came. It was difficult to celebrate anything without him.

In August, two of my friends invited me to a game night, and I ended up staying overnight. These two friends took it upon themselves to decide I should start dating again. It had been less than a year since Mike's death, and I did not feel I was ready. However, while I was showering, they created a profile on a dating app for me and started talking to a couple of guys. I was furious!

I planned to take my profile down as soon as I returned home. However, I got curious and started looking at the profiles of the men they had messaged. I noticed one of them had messaged back. I was so scared to even think about finding love and then being hurt again.

I gave the situation to God and asked him to make it very clear whether I should continue messaging or take down the profile. I then took a deep breath and sent another message.

His name was Tom. He had never been married and had no children. He was eight years older than me. He was handsome and funny. The more I talked to him, the more I liked him. He was low-key, stable, and easygoing. We also had common ground on an important issue—he had been in a long-term relationship, and she had passed away. I felt like he could understand me on a level that most others couldn't.

After two weeks of phone conversations and texting, we decided to meet for coffee and a walk at one of my favorite places—a park with a lake, walking trail, flowers, and fountains. We got our drinks and then walked over by the lake and sat down to talk. He was so handsome; I thought he looked like Richard Gere. He was also a very good listener and great to have a conversation with. After a while, I asked him if he'd like to walk around the lake. He popped a mint in his mouth and then we started walking. Our hands met and intertwined and then he stopped, bent down, and kissed me (hence the need for the mint). We continued walking hand in hand around the lake, talking and laughing.

Arriving back where we started, neither of us were ready to part ways. I ended up following him to his house where I met his cats and got a sense of how he lived. This was his family home where he had grown up and now owned. Realizing we both had things in our lives that were difficult, we wanted to lay all the cards on the table. I told him about my mental health struggles and fibromyalgia. He shared about his Meniere's disease and how that affects his life.

He tricked me that night though. He made turkey meatballs and flavored noodles for dinner, making me think he could cook. It makes me smile to think about because later I would come to find out he could only make that, spaghetti, and sloppy joes. As a bachelor, I guess he didn't need to know how to cook anything else.

The next three months we got to know each other better. He helped me through the one-year anniversary of Mike's death. I met his mom and helped her at her apartment. We visited two churches by his house (he lived an hour away). We talked extensively about how important my faith was to me. I tried to gauge where he was at in his faith, but it was difficult. When we'd pray together, I could tell he was very uncomfortable. Showing affection did not come naturally for him, and this was difficult for me to understand. At a certain point, these things just were bothering me too much to be with him. So I decided to break off the relationship. I cared for him very much and wanted to be with him. However, as I told him, I couldn't be with someone that couldn't pray for me, didn't love the Lord like I did, and wasn't able to be as affectionate as I needed.

He cried but didn't say much and let me go. The next night as I lay in bed, I thought about how disappointed I was that he was so willing to let me go—that he wouldn't fight for me. I texted him to express this disappointment. He said he very much wanted to be with me, and he would do whatever it took. I told him the faith issue was between him and God, he couldn't do it for me, and it had to be a personal decision. He said he understood.

The following week he invited me to go to a previously visited church with him. I agreed. During one of the songs, I could see he had tears in his eyes. I reached for his hand, he squeezed mine tight, and in that moment, I felt God say that things would be okay between us.

The next week, a friend's husband invited Tom to attend a men's group that met weekly to talk, study the Bible, and pray together. I could tell he was hesitant, but he agreed to give it a try. He went that first week and never looked back. Those men have become some of his closest friends and confidants in life.

In the fall of 2019, we went on a couples retreat that was unlike anything either of us had done before. We were sponsored by our good friends, Sharon and Jerry, who had previously attended this retreat. In addition to those leading the retreat, there were forty of us attending. The men slept in rooms on one side of the church and the women on the other. For three days we had no access to the outside world or clocks. (It was so weird not to be checking the time!) God's presence was evident! God brought out a side of Tom that I had not seen before. Tom even shared his faith and what God had shown him when we each gave short public testimonies at the closing ceremony.

God, thank you! Thank you for taking us out of our comfort zones and showing us that you will always be with us. Help us move beyond the thoughts and fears that plague us. Help us to take steps forward in faith believing you are by our side.

CHAPTER 21

How beautiful you are and how pleasing, my love, with your delights.
                                            —Song of Songs 7:6

*Follow God's example, therefore, as dearly loved children and walk
in the way of love, just as Christ loved us and gave himself up for us.*
                                            —Ephesians 5:1–2

On Christmas Eve that year, Tom got down on one knee, presented a ring, and proposed. I felt like everything was lined up; it was what I wanted, I loved and adored him, he knew everything there was to know about me and still accepted me, it was what he wanted, his faith was growing every day, and most importantly, I knew in my heart and soul that marrying Tom was what God wanted for me.

We began making plans for a wedding that would take place the following fall. Then a worldwide pandemic hit! My anxiety sky-rocketed. Due to COVID-19 restrictions, we couldn't even see each other in person. The whole world was on lockdown. It was unlike anything anyone had ever experienced. We did premarital counseling with our pastor via Zoom. We chose to trust God and keep our previously set wedding date.

By summer, however, my anxiety, fear, and depression all came to a head, and I ended up in the hospital again. Because of what had happened with Mike, I worried that the hospitalization might cause Tom to also want to break up with me. I had nothing to worry about though. He was so unbelievably supportive. I came home stronger and ready to be his wife.

That beautiful fall day was perfect. I could not have been happier. All the people I loved most in the world were there to support us. There were about forty in attendance, and guests wore masks inside; a little unconventional, but it worked! My two sisters were the bridesmaids, and my niece was the flower girl. Tom had a high school friend and brother-in-law stand up for him. Josiah walked me down the aisle and gave me away. Eli was in charge of the music and audio. Micah was the photographer. After the dinner, we had a party in our backyard. I wouldn't have changed a thing!

We couldn't travel due to COVID-19, so the honeymoon was postponed for a year. We took two days to just be at home and enjoy each other. Then we were back at our jobs and working on his house that we were getting ready to sell. It was difficult to be away from my new husband over the next five weeks as he spent most of his time up there until it sold. Then the day in November came and he moved in. I'll be honest—it was not all rainbows and roses! He had many years of doing things his way, had never been married before, and had never dealt with kids around all the time, especially teenagers. Plus, I was used to a certain way of doing things, especially with my boys! We had to make room for each other's opinions on everything and realize there were other ways to do things that did, in fact, work well.

One of our biggest challenges to work through was with Eli. He was very angry, did not like Tom, and had no problem expressing how he felt. As a new wife, I wanted to do things biblically —God first, husband second, kids third, and then everything else. Tom was brought up believing that boys become men who should be able to handle life on their own. Because of that, Tom and I did not agree on many issues concerning the boys. It was very difficult for me to release control to God—not Tom—but God. I had been mom and dad for so many years that I realized I had been holding the reins very tightly over my boys. I was not even letting God have his rightful place, much less my husband.

On our first anniversary, we were able to go to Ireland for our honeymoon. It was the trip of a lifetime! Upon arriving in Dublin, we picked up our rental car and realized that the international data plan on our phones had not been set up. After many calls to the carrier and being told they were working on it, we decided to get directions and headed to the hotel on our own. Needless to say, driving on the wrong side of the car, in the wrong lane, in a foreign country (with many multilane traffic circles), and without clear directions was challenging. I did not handle it well! Welcome to your honeymoon, Tom, your wife is starting out as a raging lunatic!

We stopped at a restaurant and ate our first Irish breakfast: eggs, blood sausage, ham, cooked tomato, baked beans, mushrooms, black pudding, and Irish soda bread. For two very picky Midwesterner eaters like us, it was a culture shock!

We realized if we had, had proper directions, we would have missed something special. We happened upon the old ruins of a church. They were beautiful, and our attitudes instantly became more positive. We arrived at our first hotel in Kilkenny. The staff was so welcoming, and we were happy to be at our destination. Once in our room, we could not get any of the lights to work. We finally figured out that we had to put the hotel card key in a slot in order to use the lights. We were learning so much!

Over the next eight days, we visited Killarney, the Ring of Kerry, the Dingle Peninsula, Limerick, Galway, and Dublin. We saw waterfalls, castles, the Cliffs of Mohr, botanical gardens, gorgeous historical churches, and happened upon a movie set. We met the kindest, most respectful people. The way of life there was so different from the way of life here. I never wanted to leave the peaceful feeling Ireland gave me.

God, I stand in awe of you! Time after time you prove your presence in our lives. Yet for some reason our human minds forget, anxiety sets in, and we start trying to do life on our own. At some point, we reach the end of ourselves. Then we see our need for you and cry out. Lord, I pray that each one of us would turn to you every day—in good times and bad—knowing how much you care for us and have the best plan for our lives. Thank you for being faithful, for loving us so much, and for being the same yesterday, today, and forevermore!

CHAPTER 22

So do not fear, for I am with you; do not be dismayed,
for I am your God. I will strengthen you and help you;
I will uphold you with my righteous right hand.
—Isaiah 41:10

There is no fear in love. But perfect love drives out
all fear, because fear has to do with punishment. The
one who fears is not made perfect in love.
—1 John 4:18

Upon our return home, the challenges of real life set in. My therapist recommended starting EMDR (eye movement desensitization and reprocessing) therapy to help me process the trauma in my life. She explained that since I had a good mastery of DBT (dialectical behavior therapy) skills, a great support system in place, and time (since I wasn't working full time and my kids were now out of the house), it would be a good time to allow myself to do the work of reprocessing all the trauma I've experienced. She cautioned me that it might take a while, and there may be some bad days before it got better. However, she believed EMDR would be worth the effort. She had earned my trust, knew me inside and out, and sincerely wanted the best for me. So I agreed to begin.

In February 2022 a friend highly recommended I meet with a man who had spent decades as a pastor, counselor, teacher, and missionary. Being spirit filled, he also had the gifts of healing and deliverance ministry. She had asked if I would go in December, but not feeling comfortable, I declined. However, when she invited me again, I reluctantly agreed so as not to hurt her feelings. She told me that he did not want to know anything about those he met with before the meeting. He only knew my name and that I had been suffering from depression for quite some time. He always preceded his appointments in significant prayer, trusting God to guide the session. My friend and her husband would go with us and intercede in prayer.

The day we were to go, I couldn't get out of bed. I was frozen in fear. I did not want to go at all! For some reason though, I could not get myself to tell my friend that I wasn't going. So my plan was to fake my way through it. I was crying in the car on the way there, my anxiety was so high I didn't know if I was going to survive this, and I cried out to God to help me.

The four of us walked into his home, said our hellos, and sat down in the living room. He was in his eighties, soft spoken, and very kind. He started to tell me how he opened his heart and mind to the Lord and prayed that God be in charge of what happened at every meeting he had with people. Then he told me that with many people he meets, God gives him a word of knowledge that is usually written across the forehead of the person meeting with him. He said God gave him a word for me and asked if I wanted to know what that word was. I was skeptical, but I said yes. He said the word *fear* was written on my forehead in large letters. I immediately started crying, sensing God's confirmation that he had brought me there.

We were there for an hour and a half. Throughout that time, prayer and healing took place. It was a significant step in the process of healing my anxiety and depression. I was encouraged to continue therapy and medication; but I also felt a big burden had been lifted. I was no longer afraid of what was to come, and from that night on, I began to see myself through God's eyes—as his beloved, beautiful daughter.

April brought a major breakthrough in EMDR. I felt so exhilarated by the changes I was experiencing that I convinced myself I no longer needed medication. Without telling anyone, I just stopped taking all of it. After about three weeks went by and I still felt great, I told my husband. He was rightfully very concerned, and his first question was whether I had told my therapist and psychiatrist. I admitted that I had not, and he told me I needed to immediately! I agreed.

However, another week went by before I told my psychiatrist. He was not happy that I had done this on my own without his oversight and approval. However, since I was doing so well, he agreed to keep me off the medication. He wanted to monitor me closely over the next few weeks though. I then told my therapist. She, too, was not happy and had many concerns. She, too, said monitoring was necessary and made me promise to let her know if issues started to arise.

Abba, I lift up those who suffer with PTSD due to whatever trauma they've experienced. Help each one of us trying to navigate this to get the help we need through the professionals that you've sent into our lives, the other believers who speak truth into our lives, and most importantly through a total surrender of ourselves to you. Help each one of us to heal. I speak Jesus over the negative, hurtful lies that we tell ourselves! I pray that each one suffering would get a glimpse of themselves the way you see them—that they would start to see their worth and beauty. Thank you for loving us so completely!

CHAPTER 23

For God did not send his son into the world to condemn
the world, but to save the world through him.
—John 3:17

But you are a chosen people, a royal priesthood, a holy nation,
God's special possession, that you may declare the praises of him
who called you out of darkness into his wonderful light.
—1 Peter 2:9

About five more weeks went by and then all the emotions that I'd been shoving down hit me. The anger had been building to the point where I had exploded and sworn at a drive-through worker. This was not me, and I didn't know what was happening until it was too late. By the time I went to my therapist, I was suicidal, dissociative, and beyond angry at everyone.

During my first twenty-four hours at the hospital, I definitely was not my normal self. I was throwing things, screaming at nurses, cursing or staring out a window. The hospital was not where I wanted to be, and I was sick and tired of this pattern of living. Back on medication, it took a couple of days, and a healthier me began to emerge. By the end of my stay, I knew without a doubt that this hospital was exactly where God wanted me to be at this stage in my healing. I learned so much about myself and who I wanted to be.

I met a nurse who shared how she goes through life. She said when she walks into a room, she assumes everyone will like her. If someone doesn't like her, that's okay because they are entitled to their opinion. As long as she continues to like herself, that's what matters. Her perspective amazed me because when I walked into a room, I assumed everyone, even my friends, hated me. I believed they were my friends out of obligation because they didn't want to hurt my feelings or didn't have the courage to tell me to leave. I wondered what it would be like to live like she did. I made the decision that this hospitalization would be different than any other, and I would receive all the help and healing I could.

While at the hospital, I met a young man close to Micah's age who suffered with many of the same issues as Micah. We talked privately about some of the group session topics. One of the most impactful things he said was that when he hit a wall or threw things in anger, no one was hurt except himself. I told him he was very wrong about that, explaining I've had a husband and a son behave that way, and it hurt me deeply. I told him it is emotionally abusive. He took my words to heart. He explained that he felt his mom and girlfriend shouldn't make such a big deal of his angry outbursts because he thought that hitting the wall was protecting them from being hit. I told him I could see that perspective, and I thanked him for sharing it as it helped me understand Micah better. However, I told him abuse is abuse whether it's physical or emotional; it still hurts. He left a couple of days before me. On his way out, he gave me a note thanking me and telling me how much he appreciated our talk. I appreciated it too.

I also met a man there in transition from being detoxed and suicidal to entering a long-term chemical health treatment facility. He was a meth addict. I began to realize that I was much more judgmental than I previously recognized. He didn't look like a meth addict to me; he looked like a normal clean-cut person. My assumption that meth addicts have a certain look was as silly as thinking there is a certain look to someone with mental health struggles or fibromyalgia. The truth is there can be so much under the surface of someone that we will never know unless we open our hearts and minds to see others as Jesus sees them. I realized during our conversations that I spent a lot of time trying to befriend those who I saw as morally superior, churchgoing, and successful. Jesus befriended and loved all those who needed him regardless of social status.

I shared my faith even though I didn't feel qualified. People responded positively because they could see I was nonjudgmental and real. I wasn't lying by saying that accepting Jesus makes everything in life perfect. I was telling them that although there would be trials, Jesus would never leave or forsake them. It was a true testament to how God uses broken people.

The evening before I went home, the man transitioning into the chemical health facility thanked me for sharing my faith. He said he had fallen away from God over the years, but he was rethinking that decision. He also felt he needed to tell me when he heard me say in group that I assumed everyone hated me that I should let that go. He told me he liked me from the moment we met because I'm real. He encouraged me to keep sharing this beautiful part of myself because the world needs to see it. It wasn't a come-on or a romantic kind of compliment. It was a genuine truth. I believed God's truth was being spoken through him. I knew I needed to love myself more and was determined to change.

Lord God, thank you for placing me right where I needed to be. Thank you for each nurse, doctor, and patient that I interacted with over this hospital stay. Thank you for opening my eyes to see a small glimpse of what you see in me! Thank you for teaching me what the story about the woman at the well really means. Help us to see ourselves and others the way you see us. When we can do that, there is no longer judgment—only acceptance, compassion, and love.

CHAPTER 24

In September I stood in front of the congregation at church and shared my testimony. It was as if God was holding my hand. I felt nothing but peace as I shared the words he wanted me to share.

I talked about how incredibly grateful I was for the church body that had become family to me. These people have helped me through so much over the years; they've prayed with me and for me, helped me pay bills, helped build my Habitat for Humanity home, brought meals during times of health crisis and Mike's death, helped me raise my kids, and they did it all without judgment. God has loved me lavishly through these people!

My testimony included how God has been teaching me who I am in him as well as how to trust those he's put into my life. I shared the abuse and trauma I suffered. Total willing surrender to God was very difficult because being forced as a child to surrender to my earthly father was betrayed in evil ways. Surrendering to God, however, is resulting in peace that's beyond understanding. I can now see that God has been with me all along in every situation, how he has sent people to guide me along the way, and how he wept with me in hurtful times.

I'd like to share here an excerpt of my testimony:

Just in the last year I have been able to let go of so many of the things that have been holding me hostage—The things that have been holding me back from giving my whole heart in surrender to God. I'm certainly not saying I have arrived!! I have not!! I have a long way to go but my eyes have been opened to His great love for me and that's a good start. My eyes have also been opened to the ways in which I grieve the Lord when I think so poorly of myself, His beloved daughter; when I feel so overwhelmed that it seems the only way out is to take my own life. My eyes have been opened to be able to see the past and the people in it from their perspective and situations as they were not necessarily as I interpreted them. It's been an incredible journey in forgiveness to be able to understand that we ALL do things at one point or another for those in our lives out of love that come off as invalidating or hurtful in some way but were never intended in that way. Unfortunately because of old wounds or trauma we can take an invalidating comment and turn it into something that it was never meant to be and then it is extremely difficult to let go of. After all these years of thinking I was great at forgiveness I realized I was actually just great at stuffing my feelings and being depressed. Now that it's all out there and forgiven, there's freedom. I'm learning to be assertive, create boundaries, practice self-care, and most importantly seek God's opinion on all matters.

My eyes have been opened to what is really important in life. This is hard for me to admit but I've been quite judgmental over the years. I've wanted to be a "good" Christian and hang out with the other "good" Christian women—who I had on pedestals by the way When I didn't measure up, I punished myself, told myself this is why I don't fit in with the proper high class Christian women in the church, and didn't come to church for weeks until I felt I had my act together again. When I was a single mom I wanted to hang out with the other single moms in my townhomes but I didn't want my church friends to know I was hanging out with them because I was afraid they wouldn't approve. I look back now and I think how incredibly silly. Those women in the townhomes helped me through so much. They were more accepting of me than most people I knew. In fact one woman in particular no matter how quiet I was, how many times I said no, how off-putting I seemed; she continued inviting me to things and talking to me and making me feel welcomed and I will always love her for that. God reminded me Jesus hung out with tax collectors, prostitutes, thieves, the sick, and the lame. None of us is better or worse than anyone else and I am probably preaching to the choir but I know for me I thought there was some high standard of Christianity to live up to and I was never making it and that fed hugely into my depression. I've let all that go, I've surrendered my life fully now into the hands of Jesus, and for the first time in my life I'm just being me. It feels good to just be me. I'm much happier. And I kinda like me!

Lord, thank you again and again for opening my eyes to see who I am in you! Thank you for removing the lies and replacing them with your great truth! I pray that all who are burdened with thoughts that they aren't "good enough, pretty enough, strong enough, perfect enough" would find their way to you. Please open their eyes to see how they are special, loved, beautiful, wanted, and more than enough. You love and value them so much that you sent your only Son to the cross for them! I pray these things in Jesus's precious name. Amen.

CHAPTER 25

*You are worthy, our Lord and God, to receive honor
and glory and power, for you created all things, and by
your will they were created and have their being.*
                                        —Revelation 4:11

*"But I will restore you to health and heal
your wounds," declares the Lord.*
                                        —Jeremiah 30:17

So here we are at present time (June 2023). I've been on a journey to honor God, to heal and be healthy, and to share his love with others.

My journey to honor God started at four years old when I told Granny and Papa that I wanted Jesus to live in my heart. This journey won't be complete until Jesus takes me home. Until then, I intend to do my best to honor him with my life. I very much value the privilege it is to be Tom's wife. I feel giving him respect and love as my husband and keeping God as the head and center of our marriage is of the utmost importance. There will be disagreements. There will be challenging days. But by recognizing God is in control and submitting myself to him, I will be a better wife and in turn this will help Tom want to continue being the warm, loving, supportive husband he is. This is honoring God.

I also highly value the privilege it is to be a mom. My boys have been through thick and thin with me. They've experienced things they shouldn't have had to, and I've humbly apologized for my part in those things. I am so proud of the young men they've become. They know that I will always be available to talk about absolutely anything with them. This is honoring God. I also see the blessing I've been given to be a motherly influence to the young women in my son's lives—being available to them, having open communication, and showing them love and acceptance. This is honoring God.

I learned the most important thing I can do to honor God is to spend time with him—pray, listen for his still, soft voice, read his word, and spend time in worship. Throughout the pages of this book, I've candidly shared my journey through healing and how I've found my joy. It's been a long process, and it's brought me to where I am today. I want to highlight a few tools God, the Divine Carpenter, used that were most helpful.

As I previously mentioned, DBT (dialectical behavior therapy) is a set of skills that, if applied, will provide the tools needed to cope with life's challenges. Ideally these skills would be taught to every young person to prepare them for the trials in life. These skills changed many of my thought patterns. *"It is hard to be happy without a life worth living,"* said DBT creator Marcia Linnehan. This quote opened the door to the skills that taught me how to structure my life so that it would be worth living. Although not easy—it took a lot of work—it was all worth it! This quote, by an unknown author, *"Happiness is effortful,"* reminds me that oftentimes, we need to put effort into finding joy in life.

Another DBT tool that God used in my healing process is the teaching of both/and situations. This is a problem-solving technique to help see that there can be two right answers in some situations. It takes us out of the either/or mentality and helps us look at things through another's perspective. As someone who used to live in a very all-or-nothing, black-or-white world where there was always a "right" answer, this thought process was difficult to learn (I still have to really work hard at it sometimes). Being able to see the middle ground/gray area in situations is a gift.

Although I knew my eating habits were not healthy, I was in denial of having an eating disorder. The hospitalization in 2008 forced me to address my eating disorder. After many years as a child being taught by my father how men want women to look, being shown pictures in pornographic magazines of how women should look, and being starved at thirteen because I was too "chubby," I became anorexic at sixteen. While living in New Mexico with my boyfriend and his sister, I survived on a corn dog every other day, pop, water, and alcohol. At age eighteen, I resumed eating normal foods again, gained weight, got married, and discovered my husband's pornography use.

A few years later at age twenty-two, I became pregnant and began binge eating. I would eat enough food to feel full all the time. I didn't ever want to feel hungry. Pregnancy gave me an excuse to eat. There were times I'd eat until I was so sick I couldn't get off the kitchen floor and other times I'd throw up. By the time Josiah was a year old, I felt I should lose the baby weight. This is when bulimia began. I enrolled in an eating disorder program. The eating disorder program was wonderful because I could talk to others that struggled with the same types of issues. I learned a great deal and went on to do a program through my church called Body by God. The eating disorder was under control. However, the underlying emotional reasons for my eating disorder hadn't been sufficiently addressed. That would have to come later.

In 2015, I was diagnosed with fibromyalgia and chronic fatigue syndrome. Mayo Clinic in Rochester has a fibro clinic. It was six hours a day for five days. I learned a lot about my illness; however, I did not learn the need of advocating for myself. Every time a new symptom came up, I would go to the doctor and hear some version of "It's all related to fibro." I accepted that as truth, and this became my existence for the next seven years. Then in 2022, I was introduced to my pain doctor who specializes in pain control. He was very proactive in looking at the whole body as well as its individual parts. He ordered MRI scans and neurology tests that proved there was much more affecting my body than fibro. He taught me how to self-advocate for good medical care.

EMDR (eye movement desensitization and reprocessing) first started as a way to help war veterans with PTSD. It has now been expanded to treat all who have experienced trauma by processing through those memories that hijack their lives. Normal memories are processed in our brain and then cataloged in the correct place.

However, sometimes a traumatic event is so disturbing or over-whelming that it gets stored incorrectly. EMDR helps the brain to reprocess the event. Doing this therapy has resulted in major healing. I see myself in a different light, I understand why I think or do the things I do, and I understand the perspectives of others in a new way.

Brene Brown is a writer and professor that gave a TED Talk advising listeners to be careful about "the story we tell ourselves." I could relate to her advice, but at the time, I didn't know what to do with it. Having been through EMDR, I now understand where that "story" comes from. Knowing this makes it much easier for me to change the dialogue if needed.

Expanding on trauma therapy, I would like to quote Bessel Van Der Kolk, MD from his book *The Body Keeps the Score:*

> *Trauma results in a fundamental reorganization of the way mind and brain manage perceptions. It changes not only how we think and what we think about, but also our very capacity to think. [He also says,] Traumatized people become stuck, stopped in their growth because they can't integrate new experiences into their lives. [And,] Somatic symptoms for which no clear physical basis can be found are ubiquitous in traumatized children and adults. They can include chronic back and neck pain, fibromyalgia, migraines, digestive problems, spastic colon/(irritable bowel syndrome), chronic fatigue, and some forms of asthma.*

As I read this book, I found his words fascinating, realizing I had all of these diagnoses except asthma. I now totally believe that trauma is what has caused all of these physical symptoms. The more I heal emotionally, the less pain I feel in my body, the less migraines I have, the less fatigue I deal with, and the less digestive issues I experience. It's all very connected!

God, I am so incredibly thankful for the people, programs, and therapies you have placed in my life to help me in my journey to healing and joy. Thank you for giving me the strength to do the work necessary to become the healthy person you created me to be. I pray you'll help those that are struggling with depression, anxiety, PTSD, trauma cues, and pain to advocate for themselves, do the work necessary to heal, and most importantly, find rest in you! Amen.

CHAPTER 26

*I used to pray that God would feed the hungry, or do this or that,
but now I pray that he will guide me to do whatever I'm supposed
to do, what I can do. I used to pray for answers, but now I'm
praying for strength. I used to believe that prayer changes things,
but now I know that prayer changes us and we change things.*
—Mother Teresa

*Be patient toward all that is unsolved in your heart
and try to love the questions themselves.*
—Rainer Maria Rilke,
Letters to a Young Poet

*We don't know everything, and our prophecies are not
complete. But what is perfect will someday appear.*
—1 Corinthians 13:9–10

As I close this book, I want to be clear that I am a work in progress. God is not finished with me yet! I make mistakes all the time (just ask those I dedicated this book to). None of us will be complete until the day we meet Jesus in heaven. I don't know what is to come, but I will do my best to "be patient toward all that is unsolved and love the questions themselves." What I do know is the Bible is true and "what is perfect will someday appear." In the meantime, I hold on to the amazing news that God uses broken people! I have found my joy! I've learned to forgive myself. I've learned to step into other people's shoes and try to see the world through their eyes. I've learned to try to look at myself through God's eyes because what God thinks of me is what matters most.

I'd like to give a few real-life examples of how I've applied the things I've learned to everyday life and how that's changed me. One example involves watching Eli play basketball at school. Even before leaving the car, I would begin to experience an anxiety attack. I would sit in the bleachers battling negative thoughts of what the other parents were thinking about me and our family situation. Afterward, I would cry in the car or in my bedroom. It was so frustrating because I just wanted to be a support for my son without all of the tormenting thoughts. A year after he graduated, I attended his alumni tournament. I had been putting into practice the teachings of the nurse from my last hospitalization. When I walked into that school, I felt good about myself, I greeted people without wondering what or if they were going to talk about me behind my back, and I was able to enjoy watching Eli. It was as if I was experiencing one of his games for the first time! It was a breath of fresh air not to worry about what others were thinking about me.

In a book by Morgan Richard Oliver, he writes, *"The beauty of embracing your authenticity, journey, and life is having the freedom in knowing that they don't matter. They did not create you. They cannot tell you who you are —no matter how hard they try."* Although I disagree with the statement that they don't matter because we all matter to God, what I like and can wholeheartedly apply to my life is that "they" did not create me. God created me, and only he can tell me who I am! I AM a child of God!

Another example involves a family member who I hadn't talked to in a while. I called and with noise in the background she picked up. I asked her to call me back at a better time for her, but she told me this was fine. However, every time I was speaking, she began talking to someone else. When I hung up, my initial thought was, *I guess I'm not good enough/important enough to her for her to stop what she's doing and talk to me.* However, instead of the old habit of spiraling down into more negative connotations, I was able to look at the situation through a new healthier lens. I realized that her choices don't necessarily have anything to do with me. There could've been many different reasons for the conversation going the way it did. It didn't mean that "I was bad," which is where my brain will go if I allow it to. Learning to challenge my thoughts has been extremely helpful!

The last example I'll leave you with is in regard to fear. Previously I lived in fear, not wanting to upset anyone by asking for what I needed. Then dive into despair when the fear got out of control. Now I pray, cast my anxiety on the Lord, and set healthy boundaries. Being honest with myself and others, being able to forgive myself and others, admitting when I'm wrong, and talking about how to move forward is a gift I very much treasure! One way this has played out in my life is with my earthly father. I have forgiven him for everything he's done to me. I won't ever forget, and forgiving him does not mean that what he did is okay. Forgiveness also does not mean that I have to have him in my life. There must be a boundary set to protect myself from him. What forgiveness does mean is that my heart is free from the burden that unforgiveness leaves. Forgiveness is for me—not the offender. It opens up my heart to have the relationship with God that he desires. And I no longer live in fear!

None of that means that I'm happy all the time—I'm not! None of that means that I don't take medication for my mental health—I do. What it does mean is that I've learned healthy ways to cope. I've learned that living in daily gratefulness is extremely important. I've learned that I have to put sticky notes with affirmations on my bathroom mirror and read them often. I've learned that there are times when I will not feel like reading scripture, praying, doing body relaxing meditation, going outside for walks, and other healthy habits. However, if I don't, I will lose sight of who I am. I've learned how to do things in moderation rather than being a perfectionist. I've learned that I do not need to control everything. I've learned to surrender my whole life (not just part but whole) to God! He is faithful, he is in control, he will never leave me, and he loves me beyond comprehension!

I've been through so much, and I know there will be more difficulties to come. But no matter what is happening in life, there is joy to be found! Whether it's in the flower blossoms in the spring, the changing leaves in the fall, a baby's laughter, the snuggle of a beloved pet, a delicious meal, a soft blanket, or any one of the other millions of ways God shows us he's here, there is joy to be found!

Heavenly Father, what an honor and privilege it has been to walk with you throughout the writing of this book. Thank you for giving me your words! I pray that you have spoken to the readers exactly what you have for them as they've taken this journey with me. Please help each of us to be aware of your awesome presence in the days, weeks, and years to come. Amen.

EPILOGUE

I'd like to leave you with three things that I have found to be joy killers. These three things can very quickly rob you of all joy. It's very important to guard our hearts against these things. I'm sure there are others, and I encourage you to think about the things in your own personal life that rob you of your joy. Then start going after the things that bring you joy!

1. *Worry, Anxiety, Fear.* When we allow anxiety to rule over us, we lose sight of the ONE who can calm all those fears and worries.

   "Cast all your anxiety on him because he cares for you" (1 Peter 5:7).

2. *Control* (trying to be in control of everything). We cannot control everything, so when we try, it just gives us more anxiety. When we let go of control and trust in the only ONE who does have full control, we are set free.

   "For I know the plans I have for you, declares the Lord, plans for good and not for evil, to give you a future and a hope" (Jeremiah 29:11).

3. *Complaining.* Complaining is the opposite of being grateful.

   "Do all things without grumbling or disputing" (Philippians 2:14).

"Give thanks in all circumstances; for this is the will of God in Christ Jesus for you" (1 Thessalonians 5:18).

ABOUT THE AUTHOR

Misty Dearing is a wife and a mom of three grown boys. Her passions in life include caring for the elderly, being an encouragement to other women, writing, and all things Ireland. After publication of this book, her next calling/adventure is to become a mentor to women who have experienced trauma like she has. Having dealt with many physical and mental health struggles and experienced much healing, she is outspoken about everyone being their own best advocate for good, quality care. Her number one priority is to bring glory to God for all he's done!